COPYCAT

RECIPES

Delicious Poultry and Fish Recipes,

Easy to Cook from the Comfort of

Your Home

Jason Pot

Table of Contents

1. Harissa-Crumbed Fish with Lentils & Peppers

 Preparation Time: 15 mins

 Cooking Time: 15 mins

Easy

Servings: 4

Ingredients:

- 2 x 200g pouches cooked puy lentils
- 200g jar roasted red peppers , drained and torn into chunks
- 50g black olives , from a jar, roughly chopped
- 1 lemon , zested and cut into wedges
- 3 tbsp olive or rapeseed oil
- 4 x 140g cod fillets (or another white fish)
- 100g fresh breadcrumbs
- 1 tbsp harissa
- ½ small pack flat-leaf parsley , chopped

Directions:

Heat oven to 200C/180C fan/gas 6. Mix the lentils, peppers, olives, lemon zest, 2 tbsp oil and some seasoning in a roasting tin. Top with the fish fillets.

Mix the breadcrumbs, harissa and the remaining oil and put a few spoonfuls on top of each piece of fish. Bake for 12-15 mins until the fish is cooked, the topping is crispy and the lentils are hot. Scatter with the parsley and squeeze over the lemon wedges.

Nutrition: Per serving

low in kcal 425,   fat: 13g,   saturates: 1g,   salt: 2g

carbs: 34g,   sugars: 2g,   fibre: 8g, protein: 38g

2. Creamy Fish & Leek Pie

![Preparation Time icon] **Preparation Time:** 20 mins

![Cooking Time icon] **Cooking Time:** 1 hr and 45 mins

![Chef hat icon] **Easy**

![Cutlery icon] **Servings:** 4-6

Ingredients:

For the mash topping:

- 1½ kg Rooster or Maris Piper potatoes, unpeeled
- 200ml double cream
- 50ml milk
- 50g grated cheddar
- 50g grated parmesan

For the fish pie mix:

- 100g butter
- 3 leeks, thinly sliced
- ¼ tsp ground nutmeg
- 1½ tbsp wholegrain mustard
- 100ml dry white wine or dry vermouth
- 200ml double cream
- ½ small bunch chives, chopped
- ½ lemon, zested and juiced
- 125g skinless smoked haddock, cut into large chunks
- 125g skinless salmon, cut into large chunks
- 125g raw king prawns

Directions:

Heat the oven to 200C/180C fan/gas 6. Prick each potato a few times with a knife (to prevent them from bursting) and bake on a baking tray for 1 hr-1 hr 30 mins or until soft when pressed. Cut the potatoes in half and scoop out the flesh into a bowl and mash it with a fork or ricer. Save the skins for another day. While the potato is still hot, mix in the cream and milk to make a smooth mash, season and set aside.

While the potatoes are baking, make the fish pie mix. Put a large frying pan on a medium heat. Melt the butter and cook the leeks slowly for 10 mins until they are sweet and tender, then season and add the nutmeg. Stir in the mustard, then pour in the wine and reduce until there is almost no wine left. Pour in the cream and simmer for about 10 mins until reduced by half.

Remove from the heat, and add the chives along with the lemon juice and zest. Taste for seasoning.

Stir the haddock, salmon and prawns into the creamed leeks and transfer to a medium baking dish, then top with the mashed potato, smooth over to cover the fish, and scatter over the cheeses. Bake for 25-30 mins until the cheese has turned golden brown.

Nutrition: Per serving (6)

Kcal 833, Fat: 60g, Saturates: 35g, Carbs: 42g, Sugars:6g, Fibre:6g, Protein:24g, Salt:1.2g

3. Coconut & Kale Fish Curry

Preparation Time: 10 mins

Cooking Time: 35 mins

Easy

Servings: 4

Ingredients:

- 1 tbsp rapeseed oil
- 1 onion , sliced
- thumb-sized piece ginger, sliced into matchsticks
- 1 tsp turmeric
- 3-4 tbsp mild curry paste (Keralan works well)
- 150g cherry tomatoes, halved
- 150g kale , chopped
- 1 red chilli , halved
- 325ml low-fat coconut milk
- 300ml low-salt stock
- 250g brown rice
- 100g frozen king prawns
- 2 cod fillets, cut into chunks

- 2 limes , juiced
- ½ small bunch coriander , chopped
- handful of toasted coconut flakes (optional)

Directions:

Heat the oil in a casserole dish. Cook the onion with a pinch of salt for 10 mins until it starts to caramalise. Stir through the ginger, turmeric and curry paste, and cook for 2 mins. Add the tomatoes, kale and chilli, and pour in the coconut milk and stock. Simmer for 10-15 mins or until the tomatoes begin to soften. Scoop out the chilli and discard.

Cook the rice following pack instructions. Gently stir the prawns and cod through the curry, then cook for another 3-5 mins. Squeeze over the lime and stir through half of the coriander. To serve, scatter over the remaining coriander and the coconut flakes, if you like. Serve with the rice.

Nutrition: Per serving
low in kcal 465,   fat: 15g,   saturates: 6g,
carbs: 52g,   sugars:7g,   fibre: 6g,   protein: 28g,
Salt: 1.5g

4. Greek-Style Roast Fish

⏳ **Preparation Time:** 10 mins

🕐 **Cooking Time:** 50 mins

👨‍🍳 **Easy**

🍴 **Servings:** 2

Ingredients:

- 5 small potatoes (about 400g), scrubbed and cut into wedges
- 1 onion, halved and sliced
- 2 garlic cloves, roughly chopped
- ½ tsp dried oregano or 1/2 tbsp chopped fresh oregano
- 2 tbsp olive oil
- ½ lemon, cut into wedges
- 2 large tomatoes, cut into wedges
- 2 fresh skinless pollock fillets (about 200g)
- small handful parsley, roughly chopped

Directions:

Heat oven to 200C/180C fan/gas 6. Tip the potatoes, onion, garlic, oregano and olive oil into a roasting tin,

14

season, then mix together with your hands to coat everything in the oil.

Roast for 15 mins, turn everything over and bake for 15 mins more. Add the lemon and tomatoes, and roast for 10 mins, then top with the fish fillets and cook for 10 mins more. Serve with parsley scattered over.

Nutrition: per serving

low in kcal 388,   low in fat: 13g,   saturates:2g,

Carbs: 42g,   Sugars: 11g,   Fibre: 6g,

Protein: 23g,   Salt: 0.4g

5. Smoked Haddock & Jerusalem Artichoke Gratin

⏳ **Preparation Time:** 25 mins

🕐 **Cooking Time:** 1 hr and 10 mins

👨‍🍳 **Easy**

🍴 **Servings:** 4 as a starter

Ingredients:

- 800g Jerusalem artichoke
- squeeze lemon juice
- 25g unsalted butter , plus extra for dotting
- 5 shallots , finely sliced
- 2 bay leaves
- 1 large thyme sprig, leaves picked
- 250ml double cream
- 350g smoked haddock, skinned and cut into 2cm cubes
- 25g white breadcrumb

Directions:

Peel the artichokes carefully with a sharp knife or peeler, cut them into 2cm chunks, then place into a bowl of cold water with the lemon juice to prevent discolouring. Place a large saucepan over a medium heat and add the butter. When it begins to sizzle, add the shallots and a pinch of salt. Stir the shallots to coat them with the butter and cook for 5 mins until they begin to soften. Add the bay and thyme leaves and drained artichokes, then stir to mix them all together.

Add 200ml water to the pan, bring the mixture to a simmer, then reduce the heat and cover so that the artichokes cook gently for about 10-12 mins. When they are beginning to soften, add the cream, bring to a simmer again and cook until the sauce is reduced slightly and the artichokes are tender. Season the mixture with a little pepper, then remove from the heat and discard the bay leaves.

At this point, you can chill the mixture, and finish the dish when you are ready. It will keep happily in the fridge for a few hrs.

Heat oven to 200C/180C fan/gas 6. Place the smoked haddock cubes in a gratin dish big enough to hold them in a single layer.

Pour over the artichokes and sauce, spreading the mixture out evenly. Top with breadcrumbs and a few small dots of butter. Place the gratin dish on a baking sheet and bake for 30 mins, until the top is golden brown and bubbling.

Nutrition: per serving

Kcal 531,   Fat: 40g,   Saturates: 24g,   Carbs: 25g, Sugars: 5g,   Fibre: 8g,   Protein: 22g,   Salt: 1.9g

6. Honey & Lemon Trout with Wilted Spinach

Preparation Time: 10 mins

Cooking Time: 15 mins

Easy

Servings: 2

Ingredients:

- small handful thyme sprigs
- 280g pack of 2 trout fillets, skinned
- juice and zest 1 lemon
- 3 tsp rapeseed oil
- 3 garlic cloves , 1 crushed, 2 sliced
- 260g bag baby spinach
- ½ tsp ground nutmeg
- 1 tsp honey , preferably manuka

Directions:

Heat oven to 200C/180C fan/gas 6. Cut 2 large lengths of baking parchment, put thyme in the middle of each one, then top with the trout. Mix the lemon juice with 2 tsp oil and the crushed garlic, pour over the fish and wrap up into 2 parcels, sealing in the juices. Bake for 10 mins on a baking tray.

Meanwhile, stir-fry the spinach in 1 tsp oil. When almost wilted, add the sliced garlic and the nutmeg, and continue cooking until wilted. Tear the fish parcels open, spoon on the honey and scatter with the lemon zest. Serve still in their parcels, or on top of the spinach.

Nutrition: per serving
Kcal 333,   Fat: 17g,   Saturates: 3g,   Carbs: 9g,
Sugars: 8g,   Fibre: 4g,   Protein: 34g,   Salt: 0.5g

7. Citrus-Spiked Sea Bass

Preparation Time: 15 mins

Cooking Time: 15 mins

Easy

Servings: 4

Ingredients:

- 2-3 large oranges
- zest 1 lemon (use the juice below)
- 1 tbsp olive oil
- 4 x 300g whole small sea bass, scaled, gutted and slashed a few times down each side

For the salad:

- 2 oranges , segmented
- juice 1 lemon
- 4 tbsp olive oil
- 2 bags watercress
- handful small capers
- handful pitted green olives, roughly chopped

Directions:

Finely grate the zest of 1 of the oranges and add to the lemon zest. Mix with the olive oil, then drizzle over the fish and season.

Cut the rest of the oranges into slices about 5mm thick. When the coals are ashen, arrange the orange slices over the barbecue in groups the length of each fish. Char the orange slices on 1 side, then flip them over and lay the fish on top of them – this stops the fish sticking. Barbecue the fish for 5-8 mins on each side (turning them carefully), or until the flesh flakes away easily when prodded.

While the fish is barbecuing (or beforehand), make the salad. Put the orange segments in a large bowl with the squeezed juice from the rest of the oranges and the lemon juice. Season and stir in the olive oil. When the fish is cooked, toss the watercress in the orange dressing with the capers and olives. Serve the fish with the salad.

Nutrition: per serving
low in kcal 433,   Fat: 21g,   Saturates: 3g,
Carbs:8g,   Sugars:8g,   Fibre: 3g,   Protein: 52g,
Salt: 0.9g

8. Salmon En Croûte

Preparation Time: 30 mins

Cooking Time: 30 mins

Easy

Servings: 6

Ingredients:

- 3 tbsp olive oil
- 2 large shallots , finely chopped
- 140g chestnut mushroom , finely chopped
- 3 garlic cloves , finely chopped
- juice ½ lemon
- 100g packet watercress , chopped
- 2 tbsp snipped dill
- 1 tbsp snipped chive
- 2 ½ tbsp half fat crème fraîche
- 6sheets filo pastry each about 38 x 30cm (125g total weight)
- x skinned salmon fillets

Directions:

Heat 2 tbsp of the oil in a large non-stick frying pan. Tip in the shallots and fry for 2-3 mins to soften, then add the mushrooms and garlic, and stir-fry over a high heat for another 3-4 mins, or until the mushrooms and shallots are golden and any liquid from the mushrooms has evaporated. Pour in the lemon juice – after a few seconds, that should have evaporated too. Remove from the heat, then stir in the watercress so it wilts in the warmth from the pan (see step 1). Stir in the dill and chives, and season with a little salt and pepper. Leave to cool.

Heat oven to 200C/180C fan/gas 6. Line a baking sheet with baking parchment. When the mushroom mix is cool, stir in the crème fraîche. Lay one of the filo sheets on the worktop with the short end facing you. Brush all over with a little of the remaining oil. Layer up 4 more of the filo sheets in the same way, brushing each with a little of the oil.

Lay one of the salmon fillets, skin-side up, across the width of the filo, positioning it about one-third of the way up. Season it with pepper. Spoon and spread the cooled mushroom mix over the top of the fillet (see step 2). Lay the other salmon fillet on top, skin-side down. Season again. Fold the short end of pastry nearest to you over the salmon, then bring the other end over to completely enclose the salmon (see step 3), lifting it so the join can tuck under it. Fold both pastry ends over as neatly as you can.

Brush the outside with a bit more of the remaining oil. Scrunch up the last sheet of filo, pressing it lightly on top in big folds (see step 4), then carefully brush with the last of the oil. Can be prepared 3-4 hrs ahead up to this point and chilled. Transfer the salmon parcel to the baking sheet. Bake for 25 mins until the pastry is crisp and golden. Check while it cooks and if the top starts to brown too quickly, lay a sheet of foil very loosely over it. Remove from the oven and let the salmon sit for 2-3 mins before slicing.

Nutrition: per serving

Kcal 331,   Fat: 20.2g,   Saturates:4.1g,
Carbs: 11.6g,   Sugars: 1g,   Fibre: 1.1g,
Protein: 26.6g,   low in salt: 0.47g

9. Salmon Coulibiac

Preparation Time: 1 hr

Cooking Time: 1 hr and 30 mins, Plus cooling and resting

Servings: 6

Ingredients:

- 4 eggs
- 50g butter
- 700g skinless, boneless lightly smoked raw salmon fillets (if you can't find them, use non-smoked raw salmon fillets), cut into finger thick slices
- 2 x 375g blocks all-butter puff pastry
- 1 egg, beaten, for glazing

For the rice:

- 1 large onion, finely chopped
- 1 tsp cumin seeds
- 1 tsp coriander seeds
- 4 cardamom pods
- 2 star anise
- 200g basmati rice

- 1 bay leaf
- 4cm piece cinnamon stick
- 400ml fish stock or water
- zest 1 lemon, juice ½
- large bunch dill

Directions:

First, get everything prepared. Boil a pan of salted water, add the eggs and cook for 8 mins exactly. Drain and cool under cold water, then peel and set aside.

Heat half the butter in a non-stick frying pan and sizzle the slices of salmon for 1 min on each side, just to firm up the fillets but not cook them all the way through. Lift the salmon onto a plate.

Now cook the rice. Melt the rest of the butter in the same pan. Add the onion, cumin and coriander seeds, cardamom and star anise, then gently fry for 8 mins until golden. Stir in the rice and add the bay leaf and cinnamon stick, then pour over the stock and season generously. Cover and bring to the boil, then lower the heat to its lowest setting and continue to cook for 10 mins. Turn off the heat and leave covered for 10 mins, then stir through the lemon zest and juice.

Set aside to cool. *This can be done several hrs in advance*. Once cool, stir though the chopped dill.

To assemble the pie, roll out one of the pieces of pastry to a rectangle as wide but a third longer than this magazine (23 x 40cm), then lay on a baking tray. Pack half the rice along the middle of the pastry, discarding the star anise and cinnamon as you do so, leaving a good 5cm border around the edge. Lay the salmon over the rice, then slice the eggs and lay those over the whole salmon layer. Top the eggs with the remaining rice and use your hands to gently pack everything down to a firm, even shape. Brush any stray grains of rice off the border, then brush the border with beaten egg. Roll the second piece of pastry out to a rectangle slightly larger than the first. Drape over the coulibiac and gently press the edges to seal the 2 pastry sheets together. Trim the edges to neaten and crimp with your fingers or press down with a fork. *The uncooked pie can now be chilled, on the baking sheet, for a day or frozen for up to 2 months.*

To cook, heat oven to 220C/200C fan/ gas 7.

Brush the pie all over with beaten egg and, if you want, lightly score the pastry with the back of a knife in a criss-cross fashion, making sure you don't cut all the way through. Bake for 20 mins, then reduce the heat to 200C/180C fan/gas 6 and continue to cook for 20 mins until golden brown. Leave to rest for 10 mins, then serve in thick slices with a bowl of Dill cream or Herb salsa (see recipes, below).

Nutrition: per serving

Kcal 917,   Fat: 51g,   Saturates: 29g, Carbs: 73g,

Sugars: 3g,   Fibre: 3g,   Protein: 47g,   Salt: 7.63g

10. Smoked Salmon Gateau

**Preparation Time:**1 hr and 15 mins, Plus chilling time

More effort

**Servings:** 8

Ingredients:

- 700g pre-sliced smoked salmon
- 350g full-fat soft cream cheese
- 1 heaped tsp mignonette pepper (coarsely ground black peppercorns)
- 284ml carton whipping cream
- juice of half a lemon

For the gravadlax dressing:

- 1 heaped tbsp very finely chopped shallot

- ½ tsp demerara sugar
- 50ml brandy
- 100ml crème fraîche
- 1 heaped tsp Dijon mustard
- squeeze of lime juice
- 50ml olive oil
- leaves from a few sprigs of fresh dill

To serve:
- 8 watercress sprigs
- extra virgin olive oil
- lime wedges

Directions:

Wrap the base of a loose-bottomed, 20cm non-stick cake tin with cling film, twizzling it into a knot on the underside, then slot base back in the tin. Cut the salmon into pieces about 15cm long and make a neat layer of slices, presentation side down, on the base of the tin. Start at the outside and push the slices right to the edge; after going all round the edge, fill in the centre with straight pieces of salmon.

Mash the cream cheese until smooth (a rubber spatula is good for this), working in the mignonette pepper and a pinch of salt at the same time.

Pour in two-thirds of the cream, a little at a time, and keep stirring and beating until a smooth, lightly whipped cream consistency is achieved. Now work in the lemon juice. If slightly too firm (it should be spreadable), work in the remaining cream and then recheck for seasoning.

Dollop about a quarter of the cream cheese in the centre of the salmon and spread to the edge with the spatula or a palette knife; slowly turn the tin to get an even thickness of about 3mm. Top this with a salmon layer, continuing until both salmon and cheese have been used, finishing with a salmon layer. Press the top down with your hands. Stretch cling film over and refrigerate for at least four hours – or preferably overnight. Make the dressing. Simmer the shallots, sugar and brandy in a small pan until almost dry and a deep brown colour – about 5 minutes. Tip into a bowl and leave to cool. Whisk the crème fraîche in a bowl with the mustard and lime juice, and whisk in the cold shallots.Whisk in the olive oil, trickling it slowly as if making mayonnaise.

Season, cover the bowl with cling film and chill in the fridge for 2 hours or overnight.

To turn the salmon gateau out, dip a knife into a jug of warm water and run it carefully around the inside of the tin, between the gateau and the sides, to release the salmon from the tin. Invert a flat serving plate or board on top, then turn the gateau out upside down and lift off the tin and the cling-filmed base. You will now be left with a perfectly flat top to the salmon-layered gateau.

The gateau is best cut into wedges while set firm, then left to reach room temperature for 20-30 minutes before serving – it will soften slightly and have more flavour being less cold. Just before serving, chop the dill and whisk it into the dressing, which is best served straight from the fridge. Serve the gateau with watercress sprigs drizzled with olive oil and lime wedges for squeezing. Serve the dressing in a jug.

Nutrition: per serving
Kcal 559, Fat: 48g, Saturates: 26g, Carbs:3g, Sugars:0g, Fibre:0g, Protein: 25g, Salt: 4.71g

11. Mediterranean Sardine Salad

⏳ **Preparation Time:** 15 mins

👨‍🍳 **Easy**

🍴 **Servings:** 4

Ingredients:

- 90g bag salad leaves
- handful black olives , roughly chopped
- 1 tbsp caper , drained
- 2 x 120g cans sardines in tomato sauce, drained and sauce reserved
- 1 tbsp olive oil
- 1 tbsp red wine vinegar

Directions:

Divide the salad leaves between 4 plates, then sprinkle over the olives and capers. Roughly break up the sardines and add to the salad. Mix the tomato sauce with the oil and vinegar and drizzle over the salad.

Nutrition: per serving

Kcal 140,   Fat:10g,   Saturates:2g,   Carbs:1g,
Sugars: 1g,   Fibre: 1g,   Protein:10g, low in salt: 0.9g

12. Chicken Lettuce Wraps

Preparation time: 10 Minutes

Cooking Time: 10 Minutes

Servings: 4

Ingredients:

- Lettuce leaves (for the wraps)

- Sugar (1 tsp.) Soy sauce (2 tbsp. + more for serving)

- Rice vinegar (1 tsp.)

- Hoisin sauce (1 tbsp.)

- Cornstarch (2 tsp.)

- Rice noodles (1 oz.)

- Diced water chestnuts (8 oz. can.)

- Diced green onions (4)

- Diced garlic cloves (3)

- Chili paste (2 tsp.)

- Baby Bella mushrooms (o.75 cup diced)

- Vegetable oil - divided (4 tbsp.)

- Ground chicken breast (1 lb.)

Directions:

Heat a wok using the high-temperature setting and two tablespoons of vegetable oil.

Toss in the ground chicken and cook until the pink is gone. Set aside in a covered dish for now. Pour the remainder of oil into the wok and warm using high heat. When it's hot, toss in the water chestnuts, mushrooms, garlic, green onions, and chili paste. Simmer and stir (2 min.). Return the chicken to wok. Whisk the vinegar, soy sauce, cornstarch, hoisin, and sugar. Add the mixture to the wok and cook for one more minute. Remove from the burner and set aside.

Warm one inch of oil in a skillet. Break apart and drop the noodles into the hot oil. Cook the noodles for one minute until they're crispy - not browned.

Drain on a paper towel-lined platter.

Nutrition:

Calorie: 730 kcal,   Fat: 27 g,   Carbs: 81 g,
Sodium: 2050 mg,   Protein: 38 g

13. Famous Dave's Cedar Plank Salmon

Preparation time: 15 minutes

Cooking time: 20 minutes

Servings: 4

Ingredients:

- 2 (12") untreated cedar boards
- 3 ¾ tablespoons of vegetable oil
- 1 tablespoon of rice vinegar
- ¾ teaspoon of sesame oil
- 3 ¾ tablespoons of soy sauce
- 2 ⅔ tablespoons green onion, chopped
- 2 teaspoons fresh ginger root, grated
- ¾ teaspoon garlic, chopped
- 1 ¼ (2 lbs.) skinless salmon fillets

Directions:

Soak the cedar boards for at least 1 hour in warm water. Dive more if you have time; In a shallow dish, mix vegetable oil, rice vinegar, sesame oil, soy sauce, green onion, ginger, and garlic; Put the salmon fillets in the marinade and turn to the coating. Carefully cover and marinate for 15 minutes or up to an hour; Preheat an outdoor grill over medium heat. Set the plates on the grid. The plates are ready when they start smoking and pop a little;

Set the salmon fillets on the boards and discard the marinade-cover and grill for about 20 minutes. The fish is cooked when you can scale it with a fork. It will continue to cook after removing it from the grill.

Nutrition:

Calorie: 220 kcal,   Fat: 10 g,   Carbs: 5 g,
Sodium: 320 mg,   Protein: 28 g

14. Aussie Chicken

Preparation Time: 25 minutes

Cooking time: 1h20m

Servings: 4

Ingredients:

- 4 skinless, boneless chicken breast halves - pounded to 1/2 inch thickness
- 2 tsps. Seasoning salt
- 6 slices bacon, cut in half
- 1/2 cup prepared yellow mustard
- 1/2 cup honey
- 1/4 cup light corn syrup
- 1/4 cup mayonnaise
- 1 tbsp. dried onion flakes
- 1 tbsp. vegetable oil
- 1 cup sliced fresh mushrooms
- 2 cups shredded Colby-Monterey Jack cheese
- 2 tbsps. Chopped fresh parsley

Directions:

Rub seasoning salt all over the chicken breasts. Cover and place in the refrigerator to chill for 30 minutes.

Preheat oven to 175°C/350°F. Place a large, deep skillet over medium high heat, add bacon and cook until crisp, then set bacon aside. Combine dried onion flakes, mayonnaise, corn syrup, honey, and mustard in a medium bowl. Refrigerate half of the sauce, covered. Save for later. Place a large skillet over medium heat and add oil. Add the chicken breasts in the hot oil and sauté until both sides are browned, or around 3 to 5 minutes per side. Transfer the chicken breasts to a 9 x 13-inch baking dish. Top each breast with honey mustard sauce, then with a layer of bacon and mushrooms. Sprinkle shredded cheese on top. Bake until the chicken's juices are clear and the cheese has melted, or around 15 minutes.

Garnish with parsley. Serve along with the honey mustard sauce.

Nutrition:

Calories: 813;   Total Carbohydrate: 57.1 g,

Cholesterol: 153 mg,   Total Fat: 46.1 g,

Protein: 47.2 g,   Sodium: 1807 mg

15. KFC Vegan Popcorn Chicken

Preparation time: 20 Minutes

Cooking time: 20 Minutes

Servings: 3-4 (2 cups)

Ingredients:

- Dried chunks of soy (2 cups)
- Grated ginger (1-inch cube)
- Minced garlic (2 cloves)
- Flour (.5 cup)
- Salt (1 tsp. /as required)
- Cornstarch (.5 cup)
- Vegetable broth - divided (3 cups + .75 cup)
- Breadcrumbs (1 cup)
- Garlic powder (1 tbsp.)
- Salt (.5 tsp.)
- Lemon pepper (1 tbsp.)

For the dip:

- Soy sour cream (.33 cup)
- Freshly chopped dill (1 tbsp.)
- Pepper (dash)

Directions:

Combine the chunks of soy, garlic, ginger, and salt in a bowl. Cover the chunks of soy using vegetable broth. Soak until the pieces are soft (20 minutes). Warm a pot with oil (1-inch) using a med-high temperature setting. Whisk the flour and vegetable broth from the soaking soy chunks until the lumps are removed. Add to the two bowls. Gently squeeze the excess liquid from the soy chunks using paper towels. Coat them in the bowl of the flour mixture. Transfer the chunks to a zipper-type bag with the cornstarch. Shake until coated. Toss into the second bowl of flour mixture and coat. Lastly, transfer to another zipper bag that has the breadcrumbs, garlic powder, salt, and lemon pepper. Fry in batches until golden. Drain on a layer of paper towels. Blend the sour cream, salt, pepper, and dill in a food processor to prepare the dip.

Nutrition:

Calorie: 226 g,   Fat: 0 g,   Carbs: 37.75,
Sodium: 1861 mg,   Protein: 11.2 g

16. Mediterranean Bowl

Preparation time: 10 minutes

Cooking time: 50 minutes

Servings: 5

Ingredients:

- 5 chicken thighs, skin on, bone in
- 1/2 teaspoon salt
- 1 tablespoon dried oregano
- 1 to 2 lemons, you should use the zest and squeeze
- 4 tablespoon lemon juices
- 4 garlic cloves, minced
- 2 teaspoon black pepper
- 1 1/2 tablespoon olive oil, separated
- 1 small onion, finely diced
- 1 cup long grain rice
- 1 1/2 cups chicken broth
- 3/4 cup water
- 1 tablespoon dried oregano
- 3/4 teaspoon salt

Directions:

Start by placing the chicken in a Zip lock back along with lemon juice, lemon zest, oregano, cloves, and salt. Seal the bag and keep it aside. You can either set it aside for about 20 minutes or keep it refrigerated overnight. When you are ready to cook the chicken, then preheat the oven to 350° F. Remove the chicken from the zip lock bag but don't throw away the chicken marinade in the bag. Place a skillet over medium heat and pour ½ tablespoon of olive oil. Allow the oil to heat a little and then place the chicken with the skin side down. Cook the chicken until it turns golden brown and then flip it over. Cook until the other side turns golden brown as well. Take the chicken off the skillet and keep it aside. Remove the oil and fat from the skillet. Clean the skillet using a paper towel to remove any bits that might remain. Place it back over medium heat again.

Add the remaining olive oil into the skillet and increase the heat to medium high. Add onion and sauté until it becomes translucent. Add all the Ingredients for rice and the marinade as well into the skillet.

Reduce the heat to low and allow the Ingredients to simmer for about 30 seconds. Add the chicken on top and cover the skillet. Transfer the skillet into the oven and bake for about 35 minutes. Remove the lid and continue baking for about 10 minutes more or until the rice is tender and the liquid has been absorbed. Remove from the oven and allow the dish to cool for about 5 to 10 minutes. Serve hot.

Nutrition:

Calories: 667,   Protein: 75 g,

Total Fat: 23 g,   Carbohydrate: 34 g

17. Cinnamon and Cayenne Chicken

⏳**Preparation time:** 5 hours (including refrigeration time)

🕐**Cooking time:** 1 hour

🍴**Servings:** 6

Ingredients:

- 1 whole chicken (3.5 pounds)
- ¼ cup olive oil
- 1 tablespoon kosher salt
- 1 tablespoon ground coriander
- ¼ teaspoon ground cinnamon

- ⅛ teaspoon cayenne
- 2 tablespoons roughly chopped green olives
- 1 tablespoon chopped mint, plus more for garnish
- 8 dried figs, roughly chopped
- 2 tablespoons fresh lemon juice
- 1 cup chicken broth
- 2 tablespoons roughly chopped pitted Kalamata olives

Directions:

We are going to start by removing the backbone of the chicken. To do so, place it breast down on the chopping board. Remove the backbone using kitchen shears. Use your hands to flatten it into a butterfly shape. Take a small bowl and add coriander, salt, cinnamon, cayenne, and 2 tablespoons olive oil. Apply the mixture to both sides of the chicken. Place the chicken in an airtight container and refrigerate it for about 5 hours. You can even keep it refrigerated for about 24 hours if you are planning to have it for dinner the next day. Preheat the oven to 400° F.

Take a pan and place it over medium high heat. Pour olive oil and allow it to become hot.

Gently lower the chicken into the pan with the skin side down and cook until it turns golden brown. Place the pan into the oven and then bake for about 30 minutes. Take the pan out, turn over the chicken, and add mint, figs, olives, lemon juice, and chicken broth into the pan. Place the pan back into the oven and cook for another 30 minutes, or until the internal temperature reads 165° F. You can use a thermometer to check the temperature of the chicken. Take the chicken out, transfer to a plate, top with mint, and Serve with the fig mixture.

Nutrition:

Calories: 501,　　　　　　　Protein: 34 g,

Total Fat: 37 g,　　　　　　Carbohydrate: 5 g

18.   Red Lobster's Clam Chowder

Preparation time: 20 minutes

Cooking time: 30 minutes

Servings: 8

Ingredients:

- 2 tablespoons butter
- 1 cup onion, diced
- ½ cup leek, white part, thinly sliced
- ¼ teaspoon garlic, minced
- ½ cup celery, diced
- 2 tablespoons flour
- 4 cups milk
- 1 cup clams with juice, diced
- 1 cup potato, diced
- 1 tablespoon salt
- ¼ teaspoon white pepper
- 1 teaspoon dried thyme
- ½ cup heavy cream
- Saltine crackers for serving

Directions:

In a pot, sauté the onion, leek, garlic, and celery in butter over medium heat. After 3 minutes, remove the vegetables from the heat and add the flour. Whisk in the milk and clam juice. Return the mixture to the heat and bring it to a boil. Add the potatoes, salt, pepper, and thyme, and then lower the heat to let the mixture simmer. Continue mixing for another 10 minutes while the soup is simmering. Add in the clams and let the mixture simmer for 5 to 8 minutes, or until the clams are cooked. Add the heavy cream and cook for a few more minutes. Transfer the soup to a bowl and Serve with saltine crackers.

Nutrition:

Calories436.1,   Carbs30.1g,

Total Fat 26.5g,   Protein 20.3 g,   Sodium 1987 mg

19. Grilled Chicken Tenderloins

⏳ **Preparation Time**: 10 minutes

🕐 **Cooking Time:** 1 hour 10 minutes

🍴 **Servings**: 4

Ingredients:

- 1 lb. chicken tenders or cut chicken breasts
- 1/2 cup Italian dressing
- 2 tablespoons honey
- 2 teaspoons lime juice

Directions:

Place chicken tenderloins into a large plastic bag with wet ingredients. Marinate in refrigerator for at least one hour. Add chicken and liquid to a large skillet. Cook over medium heat until liquid is reduced, and chicken is golden in color, but not dry. Be sure to turn chicken throughout the cooking process.

Nutrition:

Calories: 201,   Carbohydrates: 3g,   Protein: 24g, Fat: 9g,   Saturated Fat: 1g,   Cholesterol: 72mg, Sodium: 423mg,   Sugar: 3g,   Potassium: 444mg

20. Sunday Fried Chicken

Preparation Time: 10 minutes

Cooking Time: 20 minutes

Servings: 4

Ingredients:

- oil for frying
- 4 boneless, skinless chicken breasts
- 2 cups all-purpose flour
- 2 teaspoons salt
- 2 teaspoons ground black pepper
- 1 cup buttermilk
- 1/2 cup water

Directions:

Pour 3 to 4 inches of oil into a deep fryer or large pot and preheat the oil to 350 degrees. Prepare seasoned flour by combining the flour, salt, and pepper in a bowl. Stir to combine well. In another bowl mix together the buttermilk and water. If your chicken breasts are not fairly uniform in size place them between two pieces of wax paper and gently pound them out with a meat pounder until they are more uniform in size.

This will help with even cooking times. Pat chicken breasts dry with a paper towel. Season the chicken with salt and pepper and then dredge into the flour, dip in buttermilk, and then dredge again in the seasoned flour and deep-fry the chicken pieces in the hot oil.

Turn the chicken breasts during the cooking to make sure that both sides of the chicken are golden brown. This should take 7 to 8 minutes for each one to cook. When the chicken is done, drain in a wire rack.

Nutrition:

Calories: 503,   Carbohydrates: 51g,

Protein: 8g, Fat: 29g, Saturated Fat: 23g, Sugar: 3g

Cholesterol: 7mg,   Sodium: 1229mg,

Potassium: 161mg,   Fiber: 1g,

21. Broccoli Cheddar Chicken

Preparation Time: 10 minutes

Cooking Time: 45 minutes

Servings: 4

Ingredients:

- 4 boneless skinless chicken breasts
- 1 can of Campbell's Cheddar Cheese Soup
- 1 cup milk
- 1 1/2 cups Ritz Crackers (one sleeve)
- 4 tablespoons of melted butter (you can use more)
- 8 ounces frozen broccoli
- 4 ounces shredded cheddar cheese
- 1/2 teaspoon seasoned salt

Directions:

Preheat your oven to 350 degrees. Make can of Cheddar cheese soup mix according to package directions (one can of soup mix to one can of milk). Place chicken breasts in a 9 by 13-inch baking dish. Season with seasoned salt.

Pour 3/4 of the prepared soup over the chicken breasts. Add broccoli to chicken that has been covered with the cheddar soup.

Melt butter and combine with Ritz crackers, sprinkle buttered crackers over the broccoli. Add remaining soup mix and bake for approximately 45 minutes or until the chicken is done. (Check chicken by cutting the thickest part and look to see that the chicken is uniform in color). When chicken has been removed from oven sprinkle with shredded cheddar cheese.

Nutrition:

Calories: 1354,   Carbohydrates: 91g, Protein: 86g, Fat: 67g, Saturated Fat: 30g,   Cholesterol: 281mg, Sodium: 5234mg, Potassium: 4924mg,   Fiber: 8g, Sugar: 20g

22. Chicken Casserole

⏳ **Preparation Time:** 10 minutes

🕐 **Cooking Time:** 1 hour 5 minutes

🍴 **Servings**: 4

Ingredients:

- Corn bread
- 1 cup yellow cornmeal
- 1/3 cup all-purpose flour
- 1 1/2 teaspoon baking powder
- 1 tablespoon sugar
- 1/2 teaspoon salt
- 1/2 teaspoon baking soda
- 2 tablespoons vegetable oil
- 3/4 cup buttermilk
- 1 egg
- 1/2 cup melted butter

Chicken Filling:

- 2 tablespoons butter
- 1/4 cup chopped yellow onion
- 1/2 cup celery, thinly sliced
- 1 3/4 cup chicken broth

- 1 can cream of chicken soup
- 1 teaspoon salt
- 1/4 teaspoon pepper
- 2 1/2 cups cooked chicken breast, cut in bite-size pieces

Directions:

Corn bread mix all the ingredients for the cornbread except the melted butter together in a mixing bowl until smooth. Pour the batter into a greased 8-inch square baking pan and bake at 375 degrees F for 20 - 25 minutes or until golden and done. Remove from the oven and let cool completely. When the cornbread is cool, crumble all the cornbread and place 3 cups of the cornbread crumbs in a mixing bowl. Add the 1/2 cup melted butter to crumbs and mix well, set aside.

Chicken Filling:

In medium-sized saucepan on medium-low heat, heat the butter and sauté the chopped onions and celery until they are transparent, stirring occasionally. Add the chicken broth, cream of chicken soup, salt, and pepper. Stir until well blended and the soup is dissolved completely. Add the cooked chicken; stir and blend until mixture reaches a low simmer.

Cook for 5 minutes, then remove from the heat.

Place the chicken filling in a buttered 2 1/2-quart casserole dish or individual casserole dishes (about four). Sprinkle the cornbread crumb topping on top of the chicken mixture; do not stir into the chicken filling. It should form a crust over the filling. Place the baking dish in preheated oven at 350 degrees F for 35 - 40 minutes. The crumbs will turn a golden yellow. Serve while hot.

Nutrition:

Calories: 582,   Carbohydrates: 50g, Protein: 37g, Fat: 25g,   Saturated Fat: 13g,   Fiber: 4g, Cholesterol: 141mg,   Sodium: 2111mg, Sugar: 6g Potassium: 757mg

23. Chicken-Fried Steak & Gravy

Preparation Time: 15 minutes

Cooking Time: 10 minutes

Servings: 4

Ingredients:

- 1-1/4 cups all-purpose flour, divided
- 2 large eggs
- 1-1/2 cups 2% milk, divided
- 4 beef cube steaks (6 ounces each)
- 1-1/4 teaspoons salt, divided
- 1 teaspoon pepper, divided
- Oil for frying
- 1 cup water

Directions:

Place 1 cup flour in a shallow bowl. In a separate shallow bowl, whisk eggs and 1/2 cup milk until blended. Sprinkle steaks with 3/4 teaspoon each salt and pepper. Dip in flour to coat both sides; shake off excess. Dip in egg mixture, then again in flour. In a large cast-iron or other heavy skillet, heat 1/4 in. of oil over medium heat. Add steaks; cook until golden brown and a thermometer reads 160°, 4-6 minutes on each side. Remove from pan; drain on paper towels. Keep warm. Remove all but 2 tablespoons oil from pan. Stir in the remaining 1/4 cup flour, 1/2 teaspoon salt and 1/4 teaspoon pepper until smooth; cook and stir over medium heat until golden brown, 3-4 minutes. Gradually whisk in water and remaining milk. Bring to a boil, stirring constantly; cook and stir until thickened, 1-2 minutes. Serve with steaks.

Nutrition:

Calories: 563, Fat: 28g, Saturated fat: 5g, Cholesterol: 148mg, Sodium: 839mg, Sugars: 4g, Carbohydrate: 29g, Fiber: 1g, Protein: 46g

24. Spicy Oven-Fried Chicken

Preparation Time: 25 minutes

Cooking Time: 35 minutes

Servings: 8

Ingredients:

- 8 bone-in chicken breast halves, skin removed (8 ounces each)
- 2 cups buttermilk
- 2 tablespoons Dijon mustard
- 2 teaspoons salt
- 2 teaspoons hot pepper sauce
- 1-1/2 teaspoons garlic powder
- 2 cups soft breadcrumbs
- 1 cup cornmeal
- 2 tablespoons canola oil
- 1/2 teaspoon poultry seasoning
- 1/2 teaspoon ground mustard
- 1/2 teaspoon paprika
- 1/2 teaspoon cayenne pepper
- 1/4 teaspoon dried oregano
- 1/4 teaspoon dried parsley flakes

Directions:

Preheat oven to 400°. In a large bowl or dish, combine the first five ingredients. Add chicken and turn to coat. Refrigerate 1 hour or overnight. Drain chicken, discarding marinade. In a large bowl, combine remaining ingredients. Add chicken, one piece at a time, and coat with crumb mixture. Place on a parchment-lined baking sheet. Bake 35-40 minutes or until a thermometer reads 170°.

Nutrition:

Calories: 296,   Fat: 7g,   Sodium: 523mg
Cholesterol: 103mg,   Carbohydrate: 15g,
Protein: 40g

25. Skillet-Grilled Catfish

Preparation Time: 15 minutes

Cooking Time: 10 minutes

Servings: 4

Ingredients:

- 1/4 cup all-purpose flour
- 1/4 cup cornmeal
- 1 teaspoon onion powder
- 1 teaspoon dried basil
- 1/2 teaspoon garlic salt
- 1/2 teaspoon dried thyme
- 1/4 to 1/2 teaspoon white pepper
- 1/4 to 1/2 teaspoon cayenne pepper
- 1/4 to 1/2 teaspoon pepper
- 4 catfish fillets (6 to 8 ounces each)
- 1/4 cup butter

Directions:

In a large shallow dish, combine the first 9 ingredients. Add catfish, one fillet at a time, and turn to coat. Place a large cast-iron skillet on a grill rack over medium-high heat. Melt butter in the skillet; add catfish in batches, if necessary.

Grill, covered, until fish just begins to flake easily with a fork, 5-10 minutes on each side.

Nutrition:

Calories: 222,   Fat: 15g,   Sodium: 366mg

Cholesterol: 51mg, Carbohydrate: 14g,   Protein: 8g

26. Country Chicken with Gravy

Preparation Time: 5 minutes

Cooking Time: 25 minutes

Servings: 4

Ingredients:

- 3/4 cup crushed cornflakes
- 1/2 teaspoon poultry seasoning
- 1/2 teaspoon paprika
- 1/4 teaspoon salt
- 1/4 teaspoon dried thyme
- 1/4 teaspoon pepper
- 2 tablespoons fat-free evaporated milk
- 4 boneless skinless chicken breast halves (4 ounces each)
- 2 teaspoons canola oil

Gravy:

- 1 tablespoon butter
- 1 tablespoon all-purpose flour
- 1/4 teaspoon pepper
- 1/8 teaspoon salt
- 1/2 cup fat-free evaporated milk

- 1/4 cup condensed chicken broth, undiluted
- 1 teaspoon sherry or additional condensed chicken broth
- 2 tablespoons minced chives

Directions:

In a shallow bowl, combine the first six ingredients. Place milk in another shallow bowl. Dip chicken in milk, then roll in cornflake mixture. In a large nonstick skillet, cook chicken in oil over medium heat until a thermometer reads 170°, 6-8 minutes on each side. Meanwhile, in a small saucepan, melt butter. Stir in the flour, pepper, and salt until smooth. Gradually stir in the milk, broth, and sherry. Bring to a boil; cook and stir until thickened, 1-2 minutes. Stir in chives. Serve with chicken.

Nutrition:

Calories:274,   Fat:8g,   Cholesterol: 72mg,
Sodium: 569mg,   Carbohydrate: 20g,   Protein: 28g

27. Apple Cider BBQ Chicken Breast

⧗ **Preparation Time:** 20 minutes

🕐 **Cooking Time:** 3 ½ hours

🍴 **Servings:** 4

Ingredients:

- 1 tablespoon canola oil
- 4 bone-in chicken thighs (about 1-1/2 pounds), skin removed
- 1/4 teaspoon salt
- 1/4 teaspoon pepper 2 medium Fuji or Gala apples, coarsely chopped
- 1 medium onion, chopped
- 1 garlic clove, minced
- 1/3 cup barbecue sauce
- 1/4 cup apple cider or juice
- 1 tablespoon honey

Directions:

In a large skillet, heat oil over medium heat. Brown chicken thighs on both sides; sprinkle with salt and pepper. Transfer to a 3-qt. slow cooker; top with apples. Add onion to same skillet; cook and stir over medium heat 2-3 minutes or until tender. Add garlic; cook 1 minute longer. Stir in barbecue sauce, apple cider and honey; increase heat to medium-high. Cook 1 minute, stirring to loosen browned bits from pan. Pour over chicken and apples. Cook, covered, on low 3-1/2 to 4-1/2 hours or until chicken is tender. Freeze option: Freeze cooled chicken mixture in freezer containers. To use, partially thaw in refrigerator overnight. Heat through in a covered saucepan, stirring occasionally.

Nutrition:

Calories: 333, Fat: 13g, Protein: 25g Cholesterol: 87mg, Sodium: 456mg, Carbohydrate: 29g,

28. Green Chili Jack Chicken

Preparation Time: 5 minutes

Cooking Time: 20 minutes

Servings: 2 to 3

Ingredients:

- 1 lb. chicken strips
- 1 teaspoon chili powder
- 4 ounces green chilies
- 1 cup Monterey jack cheese
- ¼ cup salsa

Directions:

Spray a medium size frypan with cooking spray. Sprinkle chili powder over chicken. Cook chicken strips until no longer pink. Turn stove top on low and add green chilis on top of chicken. Cook until chilis are warmed. Add cheese and cook until melted on top of chilis. Put on a dish and serve with salsa on the side.

Nutrition: Calories: 516, Total Fat: 24.4g, Sodium: 697.9mg, Saturated Fat: 12.6g, Cholesterol: 209mg, Protein:64.2g, Dietary Fiber: 1.8g, Sugars 4.3g, Total Carbohydrate:8.5g,

29. Orange Chicken

⏳ **Preparation Time**: 10 minutes

🕐 **Cooking Time:** 40 minutes

🍴 **Servings**: 4

Ingredients:

- ¾ cup fresh squeezed orange juice
- 1 ½ teaspoon orange zest, grated
- ¾ cup chicken broth, reduced sodium
- 8 strips of orange peel (each approximately 2" long and ½" wide)
- 1 ½ pounds chicken thighs; skinless trimmed & cut in 1 ½" pieces
- 6 tablespoon distilled white vinegar
- ¼ cup soy sauce
- 8 small whole dried red chilies, optional

- ½ cup dark brown sugar, packed
- 1 tablespoon plus
- 2 teaspoon cornstarch
- 3 garlic cloves, pressed or minced
- 1-piece (1") ginger, grated
- 2 tablespoon cold water
- ¼ teaspoon cayenne pepper

For Coating & Frying:

- 1 cup cornstarch
- 3 large egg whites
- ¼ teaspoon cayenne pepper
- 3 cups peanut oil
- ½ teaspoon baking soda

Directions:

For the Marinade & Sauce:

Place the chicken thighs in a one-gallon zipper-lock bag; set aside. Now, combine the chicken broth together with grated zest, orange juice, ginger, soy sauce, vinegar, garlic, cayenne & sugar in large-sized saucepan; whisk until the sugar is completely dissolved. Measure approximately ¾ cup of the prepared mixture out & pour into the bag with chicken; press out the air as much as possible &

seal the bag; ensure that the pieces are coated well with the marinade. Refrigerate for 30 to 60 minutes. Bring the leftover mixture to a boil over high heat in the saucepan. Stir the cornstarch with cold water in a small bowl; whisk the cornstarch mixture into the sauce. Let the sauce to simmer for a minute, until thick & translucent, stirring occasionally.

Turn off the heat and then stir in the orange peel & chilies; set the sauce aside.

For the Coating:

Place the egg whites in a pie plate; beat using a large fork until completely frothy. Whisk the cornstarch together with cayenne & baking soda in a second pie plate until combined well. Drain the chicken in a large mesh strainer or colander; thoroughly pat the chicken dry using paper towels. Place half of chicken pieces into the egg whites; turn to coat and then transfer the pieces to the cornstarch mixture; ensure that the pieces are thoroughly coated. Place the dredged chicken pieces on a wire rack set over the baking sheet; repeat with the leftover chicken pieces.

For the Chicken:

Now, over high heat in straight-sided sauté pan or 11 to 12" Dutch oven; heat up the oil until hot.

Work in batches & carefully place half of the chicken into the oil one piece at a time; fry for a couple of minutes, until turn golden brown, turning each piece with tongs halfway during the cooking process. Transfer the chicken to a paper towels lined large plate. Heat up the oil & repeat the steps with the leftover chicken.

To Serve:

Reheat the sauce over medium heat for approximately 2 minutes, until simmering. Add in the chicken & toss gently until coated evenly & heated through. Serve immediately and enjoy.

Nutrition:

Calories:490, Total Fat:23g, Sugars:19g, Cholesterol: 80 mg, Sodium:820 mg, Protein: 25g Total Carbohydrate: 51 g, Dietary Fiber: 2 g,

30. Fish Tacos

Preparation Time: 10 minutes

Cooking Time: 30 minutes

Servings: 4

Ingredients:

- 1-pound halibut fillet, skin removed
- ¼ green cabbage
- 10 corn tortillas, warmed
- ¼ cup white onion, chopped

Salsa:

- Juice of 1 lime, freshly squeezed
- ¼ cup English cucumber, chopped

Guacamole:

- ½ bunch of fresh cilantros, chopped
- 1 tablespoon olive oil
- Pepper & salt to taste

Directions:

For Cabbage Slaw:

In a large bowl add the chiffonade cabbage together with cucumber, onion & cilantro; squeeze the lime juice on top & toss well;sprinkle pepper & salt to taste;

let sit for 30 minutes at room temperature.

Preheat your oven to 400 F. Over medium heat in a non-stick oven proof pan; heat up the olive oil until hot and then carefully add the halibut; cook until the first side turn brown; turn over & put the pan in the preheated oven until the halibut is flakey & cooked through, for 10 to 15 minutes. Flake the cooked halibut into a bowl & serve with warmed corn tortillas & the bowls of the guacamole, cabbage slaw & salsa. Enjoy.

Nutrition:

Calories: 230, Total Fat: 12g, Sugar: 2g,
Cholesterol: 15 mg, Sodium: 470 mg, Protein:7g,
Total Carbohydrate: 26 g, Dietary Fiber: 3 g

31. Chicken Fried Chicken

Preparation time: 15 minutes

Cooking time: 30 minutes

Servings: 4

Ingredients:

Chicken:

- ½ cup all-purpose flour
- 1 teaspoon poultry seasoning
- ½ teaspoon salt
- ½ teaspoon pepper
- 1 egg, slightly beaten
- 1 tablespoon water
- 4 boneless skinless chicken breasts, pounded to ½-inch thickness
- 1 cup vegetable oil

Gravy:

- 2 tablespoons all-purpose flour
- ¼ teaspoon salt
- ¼ teaspoon pepper
- 1¼ cups milk

Directions:

Preheat the oven to 200°F. In a shallow dish, combine the flour, poultry seasoning, salt and pepper. In another shallow dish, mix together the beaten egg and water. First dip both sides of the chicken breasts in the flour mixture, then dip them in the egg mixture, and then back into the flour mixture. Heat the vegetable oil over medium-high heat in a large deep skillet. A cast iron is good choice if you have one. Add the chicken and cook for about 15 minutes or until fully cooked, turning over about halfway through. Transfer the chicken to a cookie sheet and place in the oven to maintain temperature. Remove all but 2 tablespoons of oil from the skillet you cooked the chicken in. Prepare the gravy by whisking the dry gravy Ingredients together in a bowl. Then whisk them into the oil in the skillet, stirring thoroughly to remove lumps. When the flour begins to brown, slowly whisk in the milk. Continue cooking and whisking for about 2 minutes or until the mixture thickens. Top the chicken with some of the gravy.

Nutrition:

Calories: 234, Fat: 24 g, Carbs: 54 g, Protein: 61 g, Sodium: 1286 mg

32. Sunday Chicken

Preparation time: 10 minutes

Cooking time: 10 minutes

Servings: 4

Ingredients:

- Oil for frying
- 4 boneless, skinless chicken breasts
- 1 cups all-purpose flour
- 1 cup bread crumbs
- 2 teaspoons salt
- 2 teaspoons black pepper
- 1 cup buttermilk
- ½ cup water

Directions:

Add 3–4 inches of oil to a large pot or a deep fryer and preheat to 350°F. Mix together the flour, breadcrumbs, salt and pepper in a shallow dish. To a separate shallow dish, add the buttermilk and water; stir. Pound the chicken breasts to a consistent size. Dry them with a paper towel, then sprinkle with salt and pepper. Dip the seasoned breasts in the flour mixture, then the buttermilk mixture, and then back into the flour. Add the breaded chicken to the hot oil and fry for about 8 minutes. Turn the chicken as necessary so that it cooks evenly on both sides. Remove the chicken to either a wire rack or a plate lined with paper towels to drain. Serve with mashed potatoes or whatever sides you love.

Nutrition:

Calories: 265,   Fat: 47.9 g,   Carbs: 65. 5 g,
Protein: 37. 4 g,   Sodium: 454 mg

33. Campfire Chicken

⏳ **Preparation time:** 10 minutes

🕐 **Cooking time:** 45 minutes

🍴 **Servings:** 4

Ingredients:

- 1 tablespoon paprika
- 2 teaspoons onion powder
- 2 teaspoons salt
- 1 teaspoon garlic powder
- 1 teaspoon dried rosemary
- 1 teaspoon black pepper
- 1 teaspoon dried oregano
- 1 whole chicken, quartered
- 2 carrots cut into thirds
- 3 red skin potatoes, halved
- 1 ear of corn, quartered
- 1 tablespoon olive oil
- 1 tablespoon butter
- 5 sprigs fresh thyme

Directions:

Preheat the oven to 400°F. In a small bowl, combine the paprika, onion powder, salt, garlic powder, rosemary, pepper and oregano. Add the chicken quarters and 1 tablespoon of the spice mix to a large plastic freezer bag. Seal and refrigerate for at least 1 hour. Add the corn, carrots and potatoes to a large bowl. Drizzle with the olive oil and remaining spice mix. Stir or toss to coat. Preheat a large skillet over high heat. Add some oil, and when it is hot, add the chicken pieces and cook until golden brown. Lay out 4 pieces of aluminum foil and add some carrots, potatoes, corn and a chicken quarter to each. Top with some butter and thyme. Fold the foil in and make pouches by sealing the edges tightly.
Bake for 45 minutes.

Nutrition:

Calories: 234, Fat: 54. 4 g, Carbs: 67. 9 g, Protein: 76. 5, Sodium: 652 mg

34. Alice Springs Chicken from Outback

Preparation time: 5 minutes

Cooking time: 2 hours and 30 minutes

Servings: 4

Ingredients:

Sauce:

- ½ cup Dijon mustard
- ½ cup honey
- ¼ cup mayonnaise
- 1 teaspoon fresh lemon juice
- 4 chicken breast, boneless and skinless
- 2 tablespoons butter
- 1 tablespoon olive oil
- 8 ounces fresh mushrooms, sliced
- 4 slices bacon, cooked and cut into 2-inch pieces
- 2 ½ cups Monterrey Jack cheese, shredded
- Parsley for serving (optional)

Directions:

Preheat oven to 400 °F. Mix together ingredients for the sauce in a bowl. Put chicken in a Ziploc bag, and then add sauce into bag until only ¼ cup is left.

Keep remaining sauce in a container, cover, and refrigerate. Make sure to seal Ziploc bag tightly and shake gently until chicken is coated with sauce Keep in refrigerator for at least 2 hours. Melt butter in a pan over medium heat. Toss in mushrooms and cook for 5 minutes or until brown. Remove from pan and place on a plate. In an oven-safe pan, heat oil. Place marinated chicken flat in pan and cook for 5 minutes on each side or until both sides turn golden brown.

Nutrition:

Calories: 888,   Fat: 56 g,   Carbs: 41 g,

Protein: 59 g,   Sodium: 1043 mg

35. Panda Express' Orange Chicken

⏳ **Preparation time:** 15 minutes

🕐 **Cooking time:** 30 minutes

🍴 **Servings**: 6

Ingredients:

Orange sauce:

- ¼ cup flour
- 1½ tablespoon soy sauce
- 1½ tablespoon water
- 5 tablespoons sugar
- 5 tablespoons white vinegar
- 3 tablespoons orange zest
- 1 egg -
- 1½ teaspoon salt
- White pepper, to taste
- 5 tablespoons grape seed oil, divided
- ½ cup + 1 tablespoon cornstarch
- ¼ cup cold water

- 2 pounds chicken breast, boneless and skinless, chopped
- 1 teaspoon fresh ginger, grated
- 1 teaspoon garlic, finely chopped
- ½ teaspoon hot red chili pepper, ground
- ¼ cup green onion, sliced
- 1 tablespoon rice wine
- ½ teaspoon sesame oil
- White rice and steamed broccoli for serving

Directions:

Mix together ingredients for the orange sauce in a bowl. Reserve for later. Add egg, salt, pepper, and 1 tablespoon oil to a separate bowl. Mix well. In another bowl, combine ½ cup cornstarch and flour. Mix until fully blended. Add remaining cornstarch and cold water in a different bowl. Blend until cornstarch is completely dissolved. Heat 3 tablespoons oil in a large deep skillet or wok over high heat. Coat chicken pieces in egg mixture. Let excess drip off. Then, coat in cornstarch mixture. Cook for at least 3 minutes or until both sides are golden brown and chicken is cooked through. Arrange on a plate lined with paper towels to drain excess oil.

In a clean large deep skillet, or wok heat remaining oil on high heat. Lightly sauté ginger and garlic for 30 seconds or until aromatic.

Toss in peppers and green onions.

Stir-fry vegetables for 1-3 minutes, and then pour in rice wine. Mix well before adding orange sauce. Bring to a boil. Mix in cooked chicken pieces, and then add cornstarch mixture. Simmer until mixture is thick, and then mix in sesame oil. Transfer onto a plate and serve with white rice and steamed broccoli.

Nutrition:

Calories: 305,   Fat: 5 g,   Carbs: 27 g,
Protein: 34 g,   Sodium: 1024 mg

36. Shrimp with Lobster Sauce

Preparation time: 10 minutes

Cooking time: 10 minutes

Servings: 4

Ingredients:

- ½-1½ lbs. raw large shrimp, peeled/shelled, tails off and deveined
- 1.5 cups lobster broth
- ½ Tbsp low sodium soy sauce
- ½ Tbsp Shaoxing wine
- 1 tsp. of sugar
- ½ tsp. white pepper
- ½ Tbsp crushed ginger
- ½ Tbsp crushed garlic
- 1.5 cups frozen peas
- 1 bunch of scallions, sliced
- 3 tablespoon cornstarch
- 3 tablespoons water
- 2 egg whites without yolks, beaten
- ½ Tbsp of heavy cream

Directions:

Add the lobster broth, Shaoxing wine, soy sauce, ginger, garlic, sugar and white pepper to the pot. Mix well Add the shrimp. Mix well. Lock the lid. Turn the valve to Sealing. Set to 0 minutes of high pressure. Do a quick-release. Meanwhile, beat the egg whites. Make a cornstarch slurry to thicken the sauce. Transfer the shrimp to a serving plate. Set to Sauté (High) and let it boil. Add the frozen peas and scallions and mix well. When it starts bubbling, add the cornstarch slurry and mix for 1 minute. Turn off and let it cool down. When it has stopped bubbling, add beaten egg whites and stir. Add the heavy cream and give it a stir.

Serve the shrimp with the sauce.

Nutrition:

Carbohydrates:10 g,   Protein: 31 g,

Fat: 11 g,   Calories: 270g

37. Panko-Crusted Cod

Preparation time: 10 minutes

Cooking time: 10 minutes

Servings: 4

Ingredients:

- ½ cup panko bread crumbs
- 2 Tbsp extra-virgin olive oil
- 2 tsp. grated lemon zest
- ¼ tsp. salt ¼ cup light mayonnaise
- 2 tsp. lemon juice
- ½ tsp. dried thyme
- 4 6 oz. cod fillets
- 1 cup Water
- 1 lemon cut into
- 4 wedges

Directions:

Set to Sauté (High) and heat the pot.

Add the bread crumbs and sauté for 2 minutes, stirring frequently. Add the oil, lemon zest, and salt. Transfer to a plate and set aside. Mix the mayonnaise, lemon juice, and thyme in a bowl.

Spread the mixture over the top of the cod fillets.

Pour water into the pot and put the fish into the steamer basket, mayonnaise side up. Lock the lid and set to 3 minutes of Manual. Do a quick-release. Serve the fish topped with the bread crumb mixture and lemon wedges.

Nutrition:

Carbohydrates: 10 g,

Protein: 31 g,

Fat: 11 g,

Calories: 270

38. Classic BBQ Chicken

Preparation time: 5 minutes

Cooking time: 1 hour 45 minutes

Servings: 4-6

Ingredients:

- 4 pounds of your favorite chicken, including legs, thighs, wings, and breasts, skin-on
- Salt
- Olive oil
- 1 cup barbecue sauce, like Hickory Mesquite or homemade

Directions:

Rub the chicken with olive oil and salt. Preheat the griddle to high heat. Sear chicken skin side down on the grill for 5-10 minutes. Turn the griddle down to medium low heat, tent with foil and cook for 30 minutes. Turn chicken and baste with barbecue sauce. Cover the chicken again and allow to cook for another 20 minutes. Baste, cover and cook again for 30 minutes; repeat basting and turning during this time. The chicken is done when the internal temperature of the chicken pieces is 165°F and juices run clear. Baste with more barbecue sauce to Serve!

Nutrition:

Calories: 539,   Sodium: 684mg,   Protein: 87.6 g
Dietary Fiber: 0.3g,   Fat: 11.6g,   Carbs: 15.1 g,

39. Grilled Sweet Chili Lime Chicken

Preparation time: 35 minutes

Cooking time: 15 minutes

Servings: 4

Ingredients:

- ½ cup sweet chili sauce
- ¼ cup soy sauce
- 1 teaspoon mirin
- 1 teaspoon orange juice, fresh squeezed
- 1 teaspoon orange marmalade
- 2 tablespoons lime juice
- 1 tablespoon brown sugar
- 1 clove garlic, minced
- 4 boneless, skinless chicken breasts
- Sesame seeds, for garnish

Directions:

Whisk sweet chili sauce, soy sauce, mirin, orange marmalade, lime and orange juice, brown sugar, and minced garlic together in a small mixing bowl.

Set aside ¼ cup of the sauce. Toss chicken in sauce to coat and marinate 30 minutes.

Preheat your griddle to medium heat. Put the chicken on the grill and grill each side for 7 minutes. Baste the cooked chicken with remaining marinade and garnish with sesame seeds to Serve with your favorite sides.

Nutrition:

Calories: 380,   Sodium: 1274mg,   Fat: 12g,
Dietary Fiber: 0.5g,   Carbs: 19.7g,   Protein: 43.8 g

40. Chipotle Adobe Chicken

Preparation time: 1 - 24 hours

Cooking time: 20 minutes

Servings: 4 – 6

Ingredients:

- 2 lbs. chicken thighs or breasts (boneless, skinless)

For the marinade:

- ¼ cup olive oil
- 2 chipotle peppers, in adobo sauce, plus
- 1 teaspoon adobo sauce from the can
- 1 tablespoon garlic, minced
- 1 shallot, finely chopped
- 1 ½ tablespoons cumin
- 1 tablespoon cilantro, super-finely chopped or dried
- 2 teaspoons chili powder
- 1 teaspoon dried oregano
- 1/2 teaspoon salt
- Fresh limes, garnish
- Cilantro, garnish

Directions:

Preheat grill to medium-high. Add marinade Ingredients to a food processor or blender and pulse into a paste. Add the chicken and marinade to a sealable plastic bag and massage to coat well. Place in the refrigerator for 1 hour to 24 hours before grilling. Grill the chicken for 7 minutes, turn and grill and additional 7 minutes; or until good grill marks appear. Turn heat to low and continue to grill until chicken is cooked through and internal temperature reaches 165°F. Remove the chicken from the grill and allow to rest 5 to 10 minutes before serving. Garnish with a squeeze of fresh lime and a sprinkle of cilantro to Serve.

Nutrition:

Calories: 561,　　Sodium: 431 mg,　Fat: 23.8 g, Dietary Fiber: 0.3 g,　Carbs: 18.7 g,　Protein: 65.9 g

41. Grilled Sweet Chili Lime Chicken

Preparation time: 8 - 24 hours

Cooking time: 20 minutes

Servings: 4

Ingredients:

- 2 lbs. boneless, skinless chicken thighs

For the marinade:

- 1/4 cup fresh lime juice
- 2 teaspoon lime zest
- 1/4 cup honey
- 2 tablespoons olive oil
- 1 tablespoon balsamic vinegar
- 1/2 teaspoon sea salt
- 1/2 teaspoon black pepper
- 2 garlic cloves, minced
- 1/4 teaspoon onion powder

Directions:

Whisk together marinade Ingredients in a large mixing bowl; reserve 2 tablespoons of the marinade for grilling. Add chicken and marinade to a sealable plastic bag and marinate 8 hours or overnight in the refrigerator. Preheat grill to medium high heat and brush lightly with olive oil. Place the chicken on the grill and cook 8 minutes per side. Baste each side of chicken with reserved marinade during the last few minutes of cooking; the chicken is done when the internal temperature reaches 165°F. Plate the chicken, tent with foil, and allow resting for 5 minutes. Serve and enjoy!

Nutrition:

Calories:381,   Sodium: 337mg,   Carbs: 4.7g
Fat: 20.2g,   Dietary Fiber: 1.1g,   Protein: 44.7 g.

42. Honey Balsamic Marinated Chicken

Preparation time: 30 minutes - 4 hours

Cooking time: 20 minutes

Servings: 4

Ingredients:

- 2 lbs. boneless, skinless chicken thighs
- 1 teaspoon olive oil
- 1/2 teaspoon sea salt
- 1/4 teaspoon black pepper
- 1/2 teaspoon paprika
- 3/4 teaspoon onion powder

For the Marinade:

- 2 tablespoons honey
- 2 tablespoons balsamic vinegar
- 2 tablespoons tomato paste
- 1 teaspoon garlic, minced

Directions:

Add chicken, olive oil, salt, black pepper, paprika, and onion powder to a sealable plastic bag. Seal and toss to coat, covering the chicken with spices and oil; set aside. Whisk together balsamic vinegar, tomato paste, garlic, and honey. Divide the marinade in half. Add one half to the bag of chicken and store the other half in a sealed container in the refrigerator. Seal the bag and toss the chicken to coat. Refrigerate for 30 minutes to 4 hours. Preheat a grill to medium-high. Discard bag and marinade. Add the chicken to the grill and cook 7 minutes per side or until juices run clear and a meat thermometer reads 165°F. During last minute of cooking, brush remaining marinade on top of the chicken thighs. Serve immediately!

Nutrition:

Calories: 485,   Carbs: 11 g,   Sodium: 438 mg, Dietary Fiber: 0.5 g,   Fat: 18.1 g,   Protein: 66.1 g.

43. California Grilled Chicken

Preparation time: 35 minutes

Cooking time: 20 minutes

Servings: 4

Ingredients:

- 4 boneless, skinless chicken breasts
- 3/4 cup balsamic vinegar
- 2 tablespoons extra virgin olive oil
- 1 tablespoon honey
- 1 teaspoon oregano
- 1 teaspoon basil
- 1 teaspoon garlic powder

For garnish:

- Sea salt
- Black pepper, fresh ground
- 4 slices fresh mozzarella cheese
- 4 slices avocado
- 4 slices beefsteak tomato
- Balsamic glaze, for drizzling

Directions:

Whisk together balsamic vinegar, honey, olive oil, oregano, basil and garlic powder in a large mixing bowl. Add chicken to coat and marinate for 30 minutes in the refrigerator. Preheat grill to medium-high. Grill chicken for 7 minutes per side, or until a meat thermometer reaches 165°F. Top each chicken breast with mozzarella, avocado, and tomato and tent with foil on the grill to melt for 2 minutes. Garnish with a drizzle of balsamic glaze, and a pinch of sea salt and black pepper.

Nutrition:

Calories: 883,   Sodium: 449 mg,   Fat: 62.1g, Dietary Fiber: 15.2g,   Protein: 55.3 g,   Carbs: 29.8g

44. Salsa Verde Marinated Chicken

Preparation time: 4 hours 35 minutes

Cooking time: 4 hours 50 minutes

Servings: 6

Ingredients:

- 6 boneless, skinless chicken breasts
- 1 tablespoon olive oil
- 1 teaspoon sea salt
- 1 teaspoon chili powder
- 1 teaspoon ground cumin
- 1 teaspoon garlic powder

For the salsa Verde marinade:

- 3 teaspoons garlic, minced
- 1 small onion, chopped
- 6 tomatillos, husked, rinsed and chopped
- 1 medium jalapeño pepper, cut in half, seeded
- ¼ cup fresh cilantro, chopped
- ½ teaspoon sugar or sugar substitute

Directions:

Add salsa Verde marinade Ingredients to a food processor and pulse until smooth.

Mix sea salt, chili powder, cumin, and garlic powder together in a small mixing bowl. Season chicken breasts with olive oil and seasoning mix, and lay in glass baking dish. Spread a tablespoon of salsa Verde marinade over each chicken breast to cover; reserve remaining salsa for serving. Cover dish with plastic wrap and refrigerate for 4 hours. Preheat grill to medium-high and brush with olive oil. Add the chicken to the grill and cook 7 minutes per side or until juices run clear and a meat thermometer reads 165°F. Serve each with additional salsa Verde and enjoy!

Nutrition:

Calories: 321, Sodium: 444 mg, Carbs: 4.8 g, Dietary Fiber: 1.3g, Protein: 43g, Fat: 13.7g

45. Hawaiian Chicken Skewers

Preparation time: 1 hour 10 minutes

Cooking time: 15 minutes

Servings: 4 - 5

Ingredients:

- 1 lb. boneless, skinless chicken breast, cut into 1 ½ inch cubes
- 3 cups pineapple, cut into 1 ½ inch cubes
- 2 large green peppers, cut into 1 ½ inch pieces
- 1 large red onion, cut into 1 ½ inch pieces
- 2 tablespoons olive oil, to coat veggies

For the marinade:

- 1/3 cup tomato paste
- 1/3 cup brown sugar, packed
- 1/3 cup soy sauce
- 1/4 cup pineapple juice
- 2 tablespoons olive oil
- 1 1/2 tablespoon mirin or rice wine vinegar
- 4 teaspoons garlic cloves, minced
- 1 tablespoon ginger, minced
- 1/2 teaspoon sesame oil

- Pinch of sea salt
- Pinch of ground black pepper
- 10 wooden skewers, for assembly

Directions:

Combine marinade Ingredients in a mixing bowl until smooth. Reserve a 1/2 cup of the marinade in the refrigerator. Add the chicken and remaining marinade to a sealable plastic bag and refrigerate for 1 hour. Soak 10 wooden skewer sticks in water for 1 hour. Preheat the grill to medium heat. Add red onion, bell pepper and pineapple to a mixing bowl with 2 tablespoons olive oil and toss to coat. Thread red onion, bell pepper, pineapple and chicken onto the skewers until all of the chicken has been used. Place skewers on grill and grab your reserve marinade from the refrigerator; grill for 5 minutes then brush with remaining marinade and rotate. Brush again with marinade and grill about 5 additional minutes or until chicken reads 165°F on a meat thermometer. Serve warm.

Nutrition:

Calories: 311,   Fat: 8.8 g,   Sodium: 1116 mg, Dietary Fiber: 4.2g,   Carbs: 38.1g,   Protein: 22.8g

46. Classic Cheesy Italian Arancini

Preparation time: 15 minutes

Cooking time: 30 minutes

Servings: 2

Ingredients:

- ½ cup white rice
- 1½ cups chicken broth
- Sea salt and ground black pepper, to taste
- 2 tablespoons Parmesan cheese, grated
- ½ tablespoon all-purpose flour
- 2 eggs
- 1 cup fresh bread crumbs
- ½ teaspoon oregano
- 1 teaspoon olive oil
- 1 teaspoon basil

Directions:

In a saucepan, cook the chicken broth until it boils over medium-high heat. Add the rice and lower the heat to simmer for around 20 minutes. Discard the broth. Transfer the rice to a bowl. Drain the excess water and let stand for a few minutes.

Add the salt, black pepper, Parmesan cheese, and flour. Stir to combine well. Scoop the mixture out and form into bite-sized balls on a clean work surface. Whisk the eggs in a separate bowl. Combine well the bread crumbs with the oregano, olive oil, and basil in a third bowl. Set aside. To make the Italian arancini, dip each rice ball into the eggs, then into the bread crumb mixture. Press to make them firm. Arrange the Italian arancini in the air fryer basket. Put the air fryer lid on and cook in the preheated instant pot at 350ºF for 10 to 12 minutes, turning the Italian arancini over once when it shows 'TURN FOOD' on the air fryer lid screen. Remove the Italian arancini from the basket and Serve warm.

Nutrition:

Calories: 349,   Fat: 7.4g,   Carbs: 52.1g,
Protein: 15.7g,   Sugars: 2.3g

47. Pot-Roast Chicken with Stock

Preparation Time: 10 mins

Cooking Time: 2 hrs and 10 mins

Serves: 4 with leftovers

Ingredients:

- 2 tbsp olive oil
- 2.4kg chicken – buy the best you can afford
- 4 onions, peeled and cut into large wedges
- ½ bunch thyme
- 3 garlic cloves
- 6 peppercorns
- 175ml white wine
- 1.2l chicken stock

Directions:

Heat oven to 170C/150C fan/gas 5. Heat the oil in a large flameproof casserole dish and brown the chicken well on all sides, then sit it breast-side up. Pack in the onions, thyme, garlic and peppercorns, pour over the wine and stock, and bring to the boil. Pop on the lid and transfer to the oven for 2 hrs. Remove and rest for 20 mins. Carefully lift the chicken onto a chopping board and carve as much as you need.

Serve the carved chicken in a shallow bowl with the onions and some of the stock poured over. Serve with some usual Sunday veg and roast potatoes. Strain the leftover stock into a bowl and strip the carcass of all the chicken. Chill both for up to three days or freeze for up to a month to use for other recipes like our one-pot chicken noodle soup.

Nutrition:

Kcal 500,   Fat: 29g,   Saturates: 7g,   Carbs: 6g,
Sugars: 5g,   Fibre 2g,   Salt: 0.6g,   Protein: 51g,

48. Fish Pie Mac 'n' Cheese

Preparation Time: 10 mins

Cooking Time: 40 mins

Serves: 6 (or 4 adults and 4 children)

Ingredients:

- 650ml milk
- 40g plain flour
- 40g butter
- 2 tsp Dijon mustard
- 150g mature cheddar , grated
- 180g frozen peas
- handful of parsley , chopped
- 300g macaroni
- 300g fish pie mix (smoked fish, white fish and salmon)
- green salad , to serve (optional)

Directions:

Pour the milk into a large pan and add the flour and butter. Set over a medium heat and whisk continuously until you have a smooth, thick white sauce. Remove from the heat, add the mustard, most of the cheese (save a handful for the top), peas and parsley. Meanwhile, boil the pasta in a large pan of water following pack instructions until just cooked. Drain. Heat the oven to 200C/180C fan/gas 6. Tip the pasta into the sauce and add half the fish, stir everything together then tip into a large baking dish. Top with the rest of the fish, pushing it into the pasta a little, then scatter with the remaining cheese. Bake for 30 mins until golden, then serve with salad, if you like. Can be chilled and eaten within three days or frozen for up to a month. Defrost in the fridge, then reheat in a microwave or oven until piping hot.

Nutrition:

Kcal 504,   Fat: 22g,   Saturates: 12g,   Salt: 1.1g,
Carbs: 47g,   Sugars: 8g,   Fibre: 5g,   Protein: 28g

49. Fish & Chip Traybake

Preparation Time: 20 mins

Cooking Time: 35 mins

Serves: 4

Ingredients:

- 2 large sweet potatoes , cut into thin wedges
- 1 tbsp rapeseed oil
- 4 tbsp fat-free natural yogurt
- 2 tbsp low-fat mayonnaise
- 3 cornichons , finely chopped, plus 1 tbsp of the brine
- 1 shallot , finely chopped
- 1 tbsp finely chopped dill , plus extra to serve
- 300g frozen peas
- 50ml milk
- 1 tbsp finely chopped mint
- 4 cod or pollock loin fillets
- 1 lemon , cut into wedges, to serve

Directions:

Heat the oven to 220C/200C fan/gas 8. Toss the sweet potatoes with the oil and some seasoning on a baking tray.

Roast for 20 mins. Combine the yogurt, mayonnaise, cornichons and reserved brine, the shallot and dill with 1 tbsp cold water in a small bowl and set aside. Meanwhile, put the peas in a pan with the milk, bring to a simmer and cook for 5 mins. Blitz the mixture using a hand blender until roughly puréed. Stir in the mint and season to taste. Set aside. Add the cod or pollock to the baking tray with the sweet potatoes, season and cook for 10-15 mins more, or until cooked through. Warm through the pea mixture. Scatter over some dill and serve the traybake with the yogurt tartare and the mushy peas.

Nutrition:

Kcal 396,	Fat: 9g,	Saturates: 1g,
Carbs: 37g,	Sugars: 21g,	Fibre: 8g,
Protein: 37g,		Salt 0.6g

50. Herby Fish Fingers with Chinese-Style Rice

Preparation Time: 10 mins

Cooking Time: 35 mins

Serves: 2

Ingredients:

- 100g brown basmati rice
- 160g frozen peas
- 50g French beans
- 3 spring onions , finely chopped
- ½ tsp dried chilli flakes
- good handful coriander , roughly chopped
- 2 tsp tamari
- few drops sesame oil
- 1 tbsp cold-pressed rapeseed oil
- 2 large eggs
- 280g pack skinless cod loins cut into chunky strips (cut into 4 strips per loin)

Directions:

Cook the rice in a pan of water for 25 mins, adding

the peas and beans for the last 6 mins. Drain, then return to the pan and stir in the spring onions, chilli flakes, all but 1 tbsp chopped coriander, the tamari and sesame oil. Cover. Meanwhile, heat a large non-stick pan with the rapeseed oil Beat the eggs with the remaining 1 tbsp coriander. Cut the fish into chunky strips, then coat them in the egg and fry in the oil for a couple of mins each side until golden.

Remove the fish from the pan and tip in the rice with any remaining egg and stir. Serve in bowls, topped with the fish.

Nutrition:

Kcal: 487,   Fat: 14g,   Saturates: 2g,   Carbs: 47g,
Sugars: 7g,   Fibre: 7g,   Protein: 40g,
Low in salt: 1.14g

51. White Fish with Sesame Noodles

Preparation Time: 10 mins

Cooking Time: 10 mins

Serves: 2

Ingredients:

- 150g soba or whole meal noodles (300g if using pre-cooked)
- 25g toasted sesame seeds , plus extra to serve
- 2 tbsp soy sauce
- 1 tbsp oil
- 1 tsp rice vinegar (or any white vinegar)
- 200g spinach leaves
- 2 seabass fillets

Directions:

Use a spice grinder or pestle and mortar to crush the sesame seeds, then stir in the soy sauce, oil, 1 tbsp of water and a splash of rice vinegar, to make a creamy dressing, season and set aside.

Bring a pan of salted water to the boil, add the noodles and cook following pack instructions, then drain and set aside.

Using the same pan, tip in all the spinach and cook until reduced down and dark green. Tip in the noodles, along with the sesame dressing and a splash of water and toss well to heat through.

Heat the oil in a non-stick frying pan over a medium to high heat. Season the skin of the seabass, then place in the pan skin-side down, fry until the skin has crisped up and the flesh has nearly all turned opaque, around 3 mins. Flip over and fry for 30 seconds further, until the fish is flaking and cooked through. Divide the noodles and greens between two bowls and place the fish on top. Scatter over the toasted sesame seeds and serve.

Nutrition:

Kcal 624,   Fat: 24g,   Saturates: 4g,
Carbs: 54g,   Sugars: 3g,   Fibre: 7g,
Protein: 45g,   Salt: 4.1g